# START
# PLAYING
# EASIEST
# KEYBOARD

## WISE PUBLICATIONS
London / New York / Paris / Sydney / Copenhagen / Madrid / Tokyo

Exclusive Distributors:

Music Sales Limited
8/9 Frith Street, London W1D 3JB, England.

Music Sales Pty Limited
120 Rothschild Avenue, Rosebery, NSW 2018, Australia.

Order No. AM958309
ISBN 0-7119-8011-X
This book © Copyright 2000 by Wise Publications

Written by Jeff Hammer
Additional arrangements (pages 18, 19, 20, 32, 38, 43, 47)
by Sorcha Armstrong
Edited by Sorcha Armstrong
Music processed by Paul Ewers Music Design
Designed by Neal Cobourne
Photography by George Taylor
Printed in the United Kingdom by
Caligraving Limited, Thetford, Norfolk.

Your Guarantee of Quality
As publishers, we strive to produce every book to
the highest commercial standards.
The music has been freshly engraved and the book has been carefully designed
to make playing from it a real pleasure.
Particular care has been given to specifying acid-free, neutral-sized paper
made from pulps which have not been elemental chlorine bleached.
This pulp is from farmed sustainable forests and was produced
with special regard for the environment.
Throughout, the printing and binding have been planned to ensure a sturdy,
attractive publication which should give years of enjoyment.
If your copy fails to meet our high standards, please inform us and
we will gladly replace it.

Music Sales' complete catalogue describes thousands of titles and is
available in full colour sections by subject, direct from Music Sales Limited.
Please state your areas of interest and send a cheque/postal order
for £1.50 for postage to: Music Sales Limited, Newmarket Road,
Bury St.Edmunds, Suffolk IP33 3YB.

www.musicsales.com

# Contents

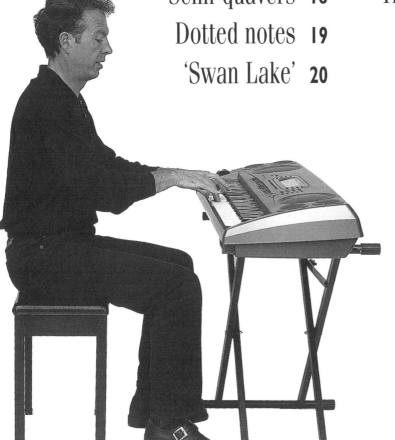

Welcome to *Start Playing Easiest Keyboard* – the easiest way to start learning and playing your favourite songs! You've got a keyboard and you're pretty familiar with its functions – you can start, stop and change the rhythms, you can select the different sounds and even pick out one or two of your favourite tunes – but that's about as far as it goes.

**So where will this book take me?**
This book will teach you everything you need to know to play all of the songs featured in The *Easiest Keyboard Collection* series, using easy-to-follow explanations, clear photographs and specially-written musical examples – all you need to get you playing, fast!

By the end of the book you will be able to read and play a right-hand melody as written on a musical stave, accompany

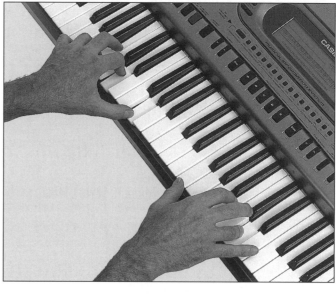

it with left-hand chords and select an appropriate rhythm and keyboard sound... plus you'll know all the right musical jargon to sound like a pro!

**What next?**
Then, we'll introduce you to some of the titles in The *Easiest Keyboard Collection* - which features pop, jazz, blues, showtunes, film and TV themes and classical pieces (see back cover for more details).

That's a lot of great music just waiting to be played so... let's get started!

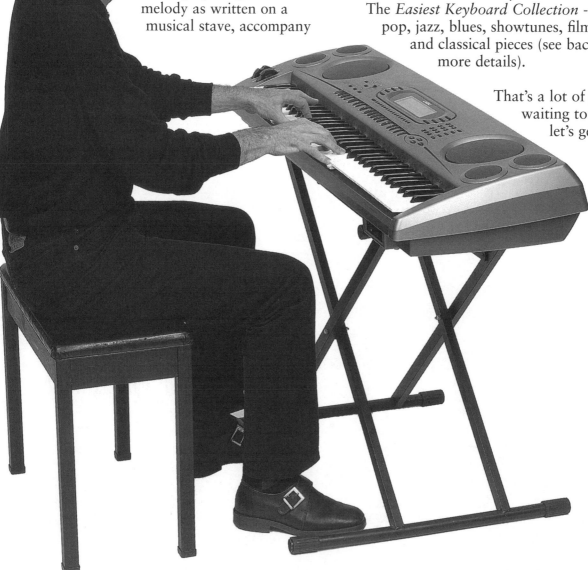

You might be thinking... 'OK, I know I've got a bit to learn about keyboard playing but just sitting at the keyboard hasn't proved too much of a problem so far!'

But the way you sit at the keyboard *can* be a problem, especially as you become more proficient and begin to spend longer periods of time playing.

## Posture

A correct playing position needs to be a comfortable one, and this means thinking about the posture of your back and the position of your arms. You need to feel relaxed as you sit at the keyboard so that your mind can be on the music that you are about to play, rather than the pain of cramp in your back, arms and wrists!

**◄ Wrong position!
Don't sit too far away from the keyboard!**

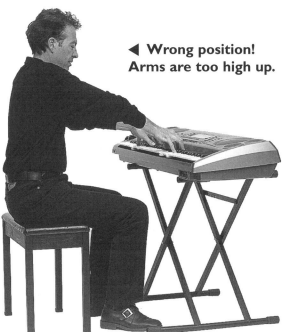

**◄ Wrong position!
Arms are too high up.**

## Your seat height

The key to this is actually the seat you choose to sit on whilst playing the keyboard.

If the seat is too high, it will force you to lean forward, which means that your back is arched forward, your arms are reaching down to the keyboard and your wrists are not relaxed.

If the seat is too low, you will be forced to reach up to the keyboard, which not only means your arms and wrists are not relaxed but also your shoulders will be tense – a situation which is far from being an aid to concentration!

Taking time to find the right seat, or using an adjustable music stool and setting it at the right height might seem like an irrelevant detail, but a comfortable playing position means you are not physically tense and the brain can communicate with the fingers without the distraction of aching muscles!

Take some time now to find the right seat and height for you – it's important to get this right first!

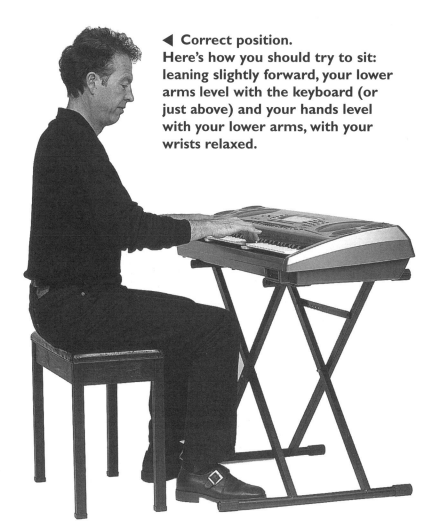

**◄ Correct position.
Here's how you should try to sit: leaning slightly forward, your lower arms level with the keyboard (or just above) and your hands level with your lower arms, with your wrists relaxed.**

# Position your hands

Now let's take a look at where your hands should be placed on the keyboard.

First, make sure that your fingers are not tense, so that they can move freely – you want your playing to sound relaxed, not stiff and wooden. A quick way to loosen up your finger joints is to curl them up to make a fist, then stretch them out again.

The correct technique is to use the tips of your fingers to play the notes whilst the fingers themselves are slightly curled, keeping your wrists slightly above the keyboard.

▲ **Wrists too low!**

Avoid playing with straight fingers – this will probably happen if your wrists start to drop below the level of the keyboard, also making it difficult to use your fingertips to actually play the notes.

▲ **Wrists too high, fingers stiff!**

Make sure that your wrists are not too high above the keyboard – you'll just be playing with the tips of your fingers. Check your seat height again!

◀ **Good technique**

Remember to keep your hands and wrists relaxed, with your fingers slightly curled, hovering above the keys.

In order to play the keyboard, your fingers will need to be loose, supple and able to move freely, and this applies particularly to the right hand which plays the melody line.

In order to achieve this you will need to warm up and exercise your fingers, just like an athlete training on the track for the big race – except you can stay at home and use the dining-room table!

You will need to be able to move your fingers freely and independently of each other, so that they can easily move around the keyboard and play the various notes of a tune.

Number your fingers as shown in the diagram below. Now try moving the fingers from 1-2, 1-2-3 (etc), as if practising on the keyboard but actually using the table!

Keep trying this until your fingers are moving smoothly and any stiffness has gone and then move on and add another finger.

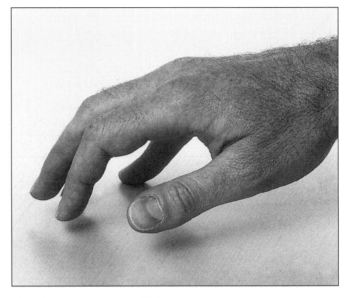

▲ **It's always a good idea to use some warm-up techniques such as these before you play – whether it's on the table or on the keyboard!**

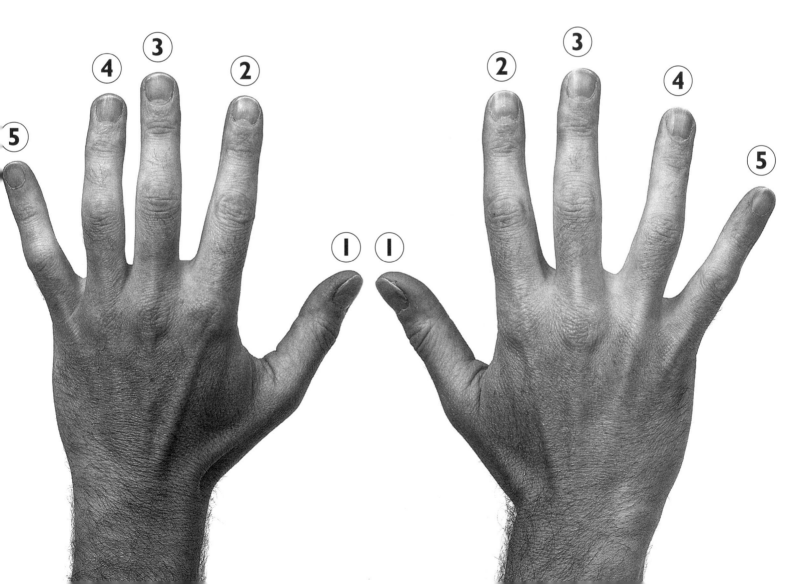

Now that your fingers are moving smoothly it is time to start playing actual notes on your keyboard.

This means that accuracy (or playing the correct notes) now needs to be taken into account – and being able to play individual notes cleanly and accurately is obviously a fundamental skill of keyboard playing.

**Correct position**

The photo (right) shows the fingers of a right hand correctly positioned over five notes of the keyboard, with the thumb on middle C.

Find this position on your keyboard and place your fingers on the notes so that you start to get the feel of the way the notes are spaced.

Now try moving the fingers on the keyboard in the same way as you did on the table (1-2, 1-2, 1-2-3, 1-2-3, 1-2-3-4, 1-2-3-4, etc), making sure your fingers are moving smoothly and accurately.

It might be worth leaving the keyboard switched off or at least wearing headphones to start with!

You're now playing the keyboard: what you need to know now is which notes you are actually playing.

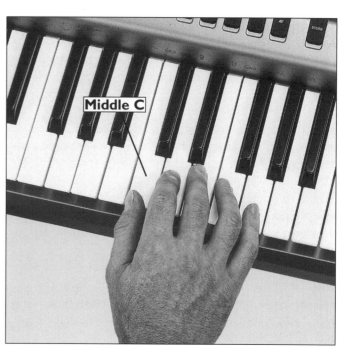

▲ **Here's a good place to start – middle C.**

▲ **Now move the three fingers marked over the white keys, starting with middle C.**

◀ **Try to remember to keep your wrists relaxed, not too high or low, and your fingers supple.**

## HINTS & TIPS

**Middle C** *is generally the C closest to the centre of the keyboard. We use it as a reference point for both the right and left hands.*

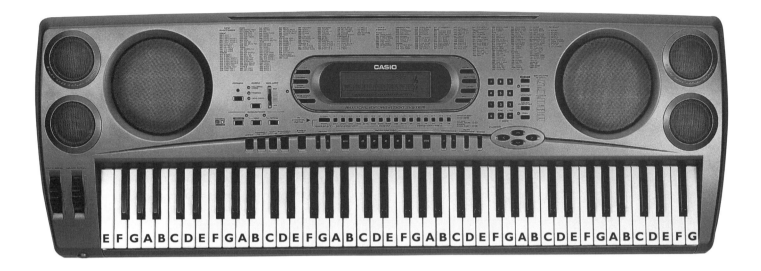

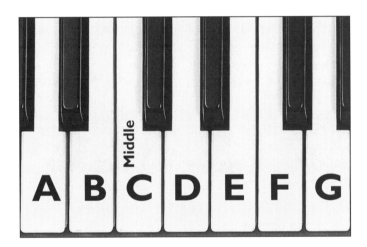

The keyboard is made up of white and black notes with the note furthest to the left being the lowest in pitch and the note furthest to the right the highest in pitch.

Given the number of different notes it might seem a daunting task to have to remember which one is which, but look a bit closer and you'll find that the same series of twelve white and black notes is repeated across the length of the keyboard. The black notes alternate in groups of two and three which helps to identify the various white notes which are named A to G.

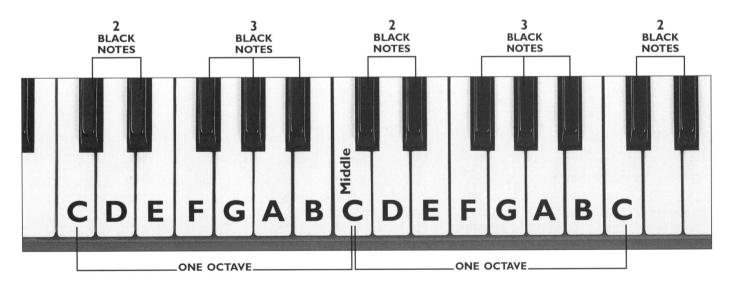

## The octave

As we said before, the same series of 12 notes is repeated across the keyboard – and each series of 12 notes is called an **octave**, e.g. C – C, G – G. The only thing that differs is the pitch of the repeated note which will be higher or lower depending on which direction you are moving across the keyboard.

### HINTS & TIPS

To find **middle C** quickly, look for the groups of two black notes. The note to the left is C, and the C closest to the centre of the keyboard is middle C.

Although we've seen that the keyboard is made up of a repeating series of **octaves**, being able to find notes quickly and easily is clearly vital to keyboard playing. It's a good idea to spend a little time getting used to the names and positions of all the notes. The quicker you recognise them, the easier it will be to follow a piece of music.

**Exercises**

Here are a couple of easy exercises for you to try, to help you get used to finding notes on the keyboard. You can use the diagram if you are unsure of which notes to play.

▼ **Try to find these notes: C, E and G. Start with middle C, and work from there.**

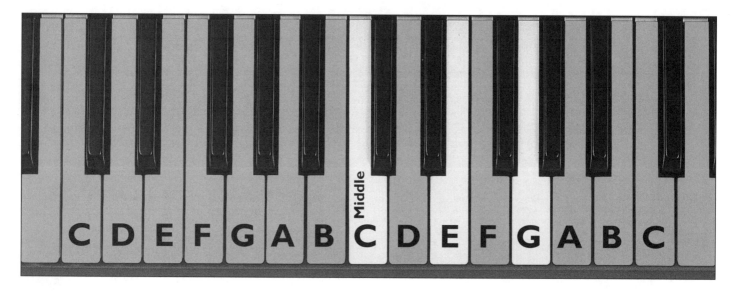

▼ **Now for something a bit harder. Try and find D, F and A in the octave above middle C.**

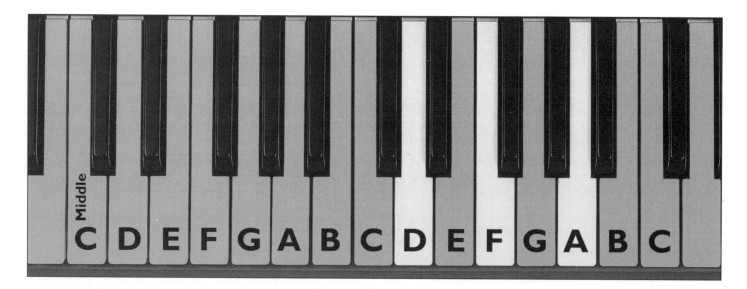

**HINTS & TIPS**

*Find **middle C** first, then the C above it. The starting note is next to C, on the right. Have a look at the diagram if you need more help.*

To the untrained eye, written music looks extremely complex: all sorts of different notes - some with stalks, others with little tails, some filled in, others joined together – lots of strange symbols and all written on blocks of five horizontal lines.

## HINTS & TIPS

*Being able to translate what you see on the page to the notes on the keyboard is a fundamental skill of keyboard playing.*

### The stave

The block of five horizontal lines on which the notes are written is called a **stave** and each line or space between the lines represents a note on the keyboard.

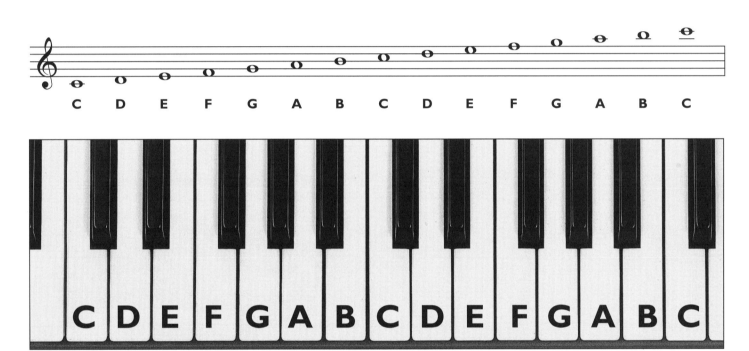

▲ **The notes marked on this keyboard correspond with the diagram of the scale of C above.**

### ▼ Exercise

Try finding the right notes on your keyboard from this piece of music. The names of the notes are printed under the stave but try covering them up at first and then use them to check you are right later.

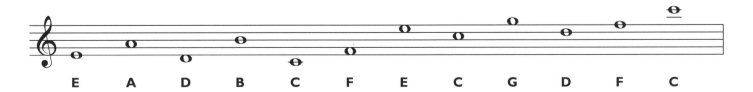

# Introducing rhythm

Now you know some note names, you might be asking... how long do I play the notes for?

## ⁴/₄ Rhythm

Most music has a steady beat and these beats are grouped together into bars. These are simply groups of notes separated by vertical lines called **bar-lines**. The most common way to group these beats is into fours, i.e. four beats in a bar, which is referred to as ⁴/₄ and is written at the beginning of a piece of music.

## Note lengths

The way each note is written tells you how long to play it for - the first notes we're going to look at are the 4-beat, 2-beat, and 1-beat notes.

## The semi-breve

The semi-breve (or whole note) lasts for four beats, which is the length of a whole bar in ⁴/₄ time:

1 - 2 - 3 - 4      1 - 2 - 3 - 4

## The minim

The minim (or half-note) lasts for two beats:

1 - 2 - 3 - 4      1 - 2 - 3 - 4

## The crotchet

The crotchet (or quarter note) lasts for one beat:

1 - 2 - 3 - 4      1 - 2 - 3 - 4

## JARGON BUSTER

**Bar** *or* **Measure?**
*These are the same thing. Bar is used in Britain, whereas in continental Europe and America it is referred to as a measure.*

## HINTS & TIPS

*The technical term for a marking such as ⁴/₄ is* **time signature***, but more about that later.*

## The metronome

A metronome is a very useful device, especially when you're trying to count time. There are various different types – the old 'pendulum' style, which makes a noise like a clock ticking, or the more recent electronic kind (pictured below) which beeps.

Simply set the speed you want the music to go (i.e. 120) and it will beep 120 times per minute. If you're in ⁴/₄, then it will count **crotchets** for you.

▼ **A modern electronic metronome**

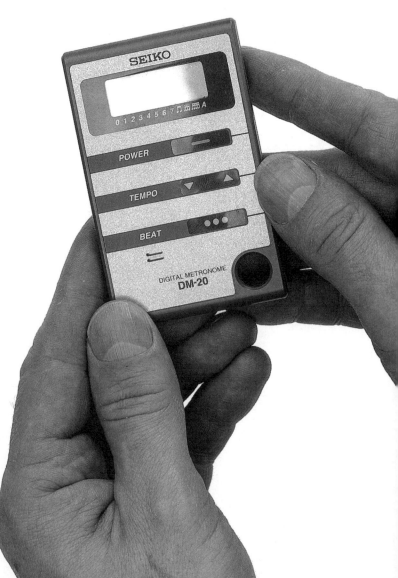

# The use of counting

We're not talking about doing your times tables here! Using a steady beat (or 'counting') is vital in music, to make sure you play notes for the right length – and at the right speed.

The count for 4/4 is simply...

**1-2-3-4/ 1-2-3-4/ 1-2-3-4/** etc.

Each count of 1 is the start of a new bar. Try to keep your counting steady – i.e. don't speed up or slow down.

Play the following notes paying particular attention to the number of beats each note is worth – using a steady count will emphasise the difference between each note.

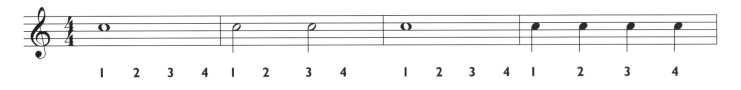

Now that you can read the notes on a music stave and know how many beats each note is worth you are already at the stage where you can start playing some music from a score!

## HINTS & TIPS

*A good habit to get into is to start a steady count before you actually begin the piece and then keep to that speed, rather than slowing down and speeding up depending on the difficulty of the bar you are currently playing!*

▼ **Exercise**
Try this piece of music which features everything you've learnt so far...

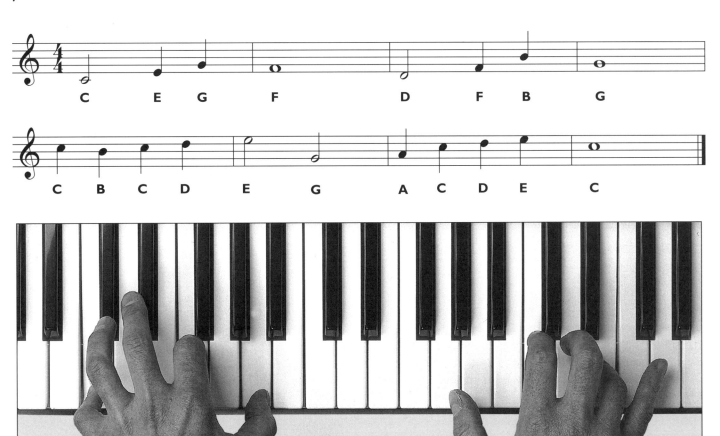

# Sharps and flats

**M**ost pieces of music don't actually use every note available on the stave because popular music is based on **scales**.

The most common type of scale is the **major** scale. You should be familiar with the names of each of the note names used in the following scales.

### C major scale
Try playing these notes which make up the scale of C major:

C  D  E  F  G  A  B  C

### D major scale
You will have noticed that all the notes you played were white notes. Now try a similar progression of white notes, but this time, starting on **D**:

D  E  F  G  A  B  C  D

Your ears should be telling you that this doesn't sound the same as the scale of **C major**! The simple reason for this is that the spacing between the notes is not the same due to the unequal grouping of the black notes on the keyboard. In order to produce a major scale starting on **D** you will have to start using the black notes.

### Sharps
Black notes are given the same letter names as the white notes on the keyboard. If they are to the right of the white note (in other words are higher in pitch) they are called **sharp** and are written like this:

F♯ or    C♯ or    G♯ or    D♯ or
F sharp   C sharp   G sharp   D sharp

### Flats
If the black notes are to the left of the white note (in other words lower in pitch) they are called **flat** and are written like this:

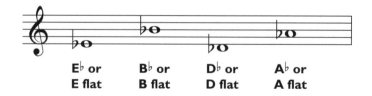

E♭ or    B♭ or    D♭ or    A♭ or
E flat   B flat   D flat   A flat

### Naturals
One other accidental you need to become familiar with is the **natural**. This sign ( ♮ ) is used to indicate a note which is neither sharp nor flat. When it's used in front of a note, it cancels a previous accidental.

Let's try the scale starting on **D** again but this time using some black notes, in this instance **sharps**:

This now has a similar sound to the scale of **C major** but simply starts one note higher.

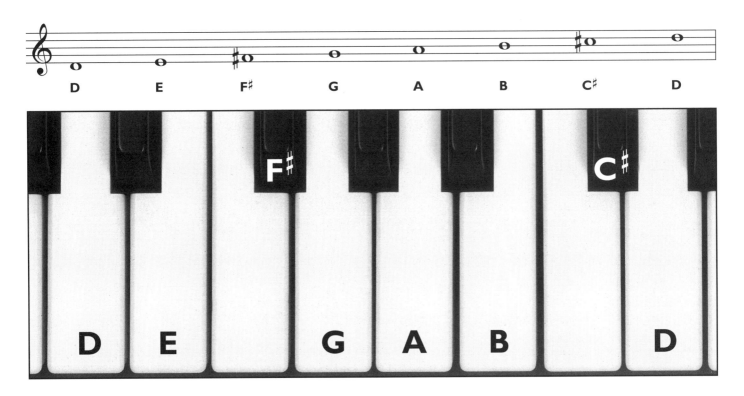

A major scale starting on **F** would also need to use black notes – but this time we use a **flat**:

A piece of music is usually referred to as being 'in' a certain key – so when you hear someone say 'Let's try this one in **G major**', that doesn't limit the notes to the scale of **G**, but it does mean that these notes will mostly feature in the song.

To avoid having to constantly add a sharp or flat to the notes when writing a piece of music, a **key signature** is added at the beginning of the piece, which simply means that whenever you come across this note, play it as a sharp or flat.

**Scale of D**

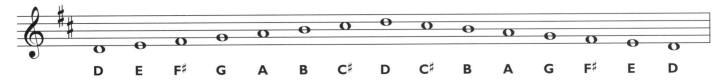

**Scale of F**

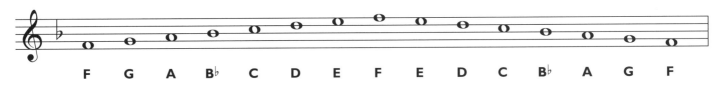

This means that the music doesn't need to have so many ♯ and ♭ symbols written on the stave, which makes it less complicated-looking.

# Key signatures (continued)

Don't forget to look at the key signature at the beginning of the piece, and pay particular attention to the extra sharps (accidentals). Here's a piece designed to get you thinking about using sharps, and also playing the black notes on the keyboard.

Remember that in addition to the sharps marked in the music, all **F**s and **C**s should be played as **F♯**s and **C♯**s, because of the key signature.

Watch out for the naturals!

**Try this**

Now try this tune which also makes use of black notes but this time, written as flats. As before, don't forget to take note of the key signature.

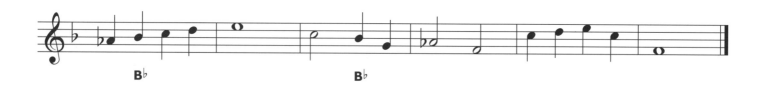

The notes we've looked at so far all have a value measured in whole beats, i.e. a **semi-breve** = 4 beats, a **minim** = 2 beats and a **crotchet** = 1 beat.

However, in order to play faster rhythms you will have to play notes between the beats of a bar. Notes with values of less than a beat have tails on their stems and a **quaver** looks like this:

quaver ▶

A **quaver** has a value of half a crotchet, so...

quaver      +      quaver      =      crotchet

## HINTS & TIPS

*On their own, quavers are written with a curved **flag**, or **tail**, attached to the stem, but when there are two or more quavers together in a row, they are bracketed together with a **beam** to make them easier to read.*

**One quaver**

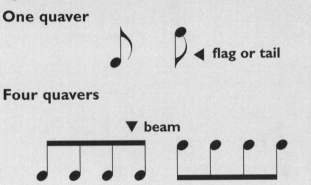

◀ flag or tail

**Four quavers**

▼ beam

If there are four **crotchets** in a bar they are counted like this:

If we change the **crotchets** to **quavers** there will be eight in a bar and this time the counting goes like this:

Try playing this tune which features **quavers** as well as the other notes you have already looked at. Remember, each bar should add up to 4 beats.

# Semi-quavers

To play even faster rhythms will involve playing **semi-quavers**. A semi-quaver can be recognised by the two tails it has on its stem and it looks like this...

◄ semi-quaver

The **semi-quaver** has a value of a quarter of a beat so...

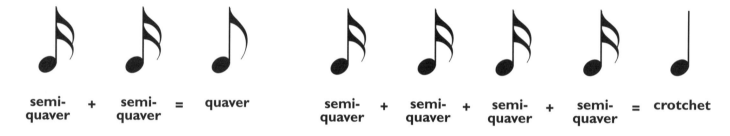

semi-quaver + semi-quaver = quaver     semi-quaver + semi-quaver + semi-quaver + semi-quaver = crotchet

There are therefore sixteen **semi-quavers** in a ⁴/₄ bar and they are counted like this...

1 - a-and-a  2 - a-and-a  3 - a-and-a  4 - a-and-a     1 - a-and-a  2 - a-and-a  3 - a-and-a  4 - a-and-a

Now try this well-known piece which uses **semi-quavers** in a variety of different ways. We've added numbers under the notes to indicate how you should count. Start slowly, but aim for accuracy. You'll soon be able to build up speed!

**Extract from William Tell Overture**
by Gioachino Rossini

So far, we have looked at a wide range of rhythms and note values – from the four beats of a **semi-breve** through to the quarter-beats of a **semi-quaver**.

We are now going to look at **dotted** notes, which move us away from playing regimented rhythms and begin to introduce rhythms which are more **syncopated**.

## Dotted note values

A dot after a note simply adds another half of that note's value to it. For example, a dotted **minim** is made up of a **minim** and a **crotchet**, making a note worth 3 beats. Have a look at the diagram on the right, to become familiar with these notes.

Usually, dotted notes are followed by another 'half-length' note, in order to make up an even beat. For example, a dotted **quaver** will frequently be followed by a **semi-quaver**, in order to make up one full beat.

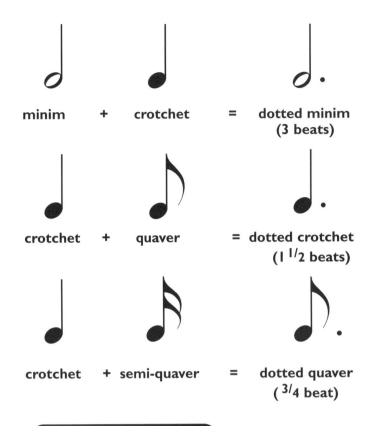

minim + crotchet = dotted minim (3 beats)

crotchet + quaver = dotted crotchet (1 $\frac{1}{2}$ beats)

crotchet + semi-quaver = dotted quaver ($\frac{3}{4}$ beat)

### ▼ Exercise

Now have a look at the example below - another popular piece. This time, we haven't given counts under the notes: why not fill these in yourself? Or, better still, try doing it without writing the counts in.

## HINTS & TIPS

*The word **syncopated** simply means rhythms which are placed on the off-beat, or weak beats i.e. beat 2 or 4. Adding dots to notes adds to the rhythmic effect.*

## Extract from Symphony No. 9 – 'New World'

Op. 95, 4th movement. By Antonin Dvořák

#  Swan Lake

**H**ere's what you've learned already:

- **The correct playing position**
- **Finding notes on the keyboard**
- **Reading notes from a piece of music**
- **Note values from semi-breve to semi-quaver**
- **Dotted notes**
- **Sharps and flats**

You now have a chance to play a well-known classical piece, which will bring together all of the elements you've learned already. It's a chance to see just how far you've already progressed with your keyboard playing.

Remember to count, and start slowly, building up to the speed indicated. Why not try a string sound for this piece (see page 44)?

**Extract from 'Swan Lake'**

by Piotr Ilyich Tchaikovsky

So far we've looked at a number of different notes and their durations.

However, music doesn't only consist of making sounds, it also involves *not* making sounds i.e. silence. Just as a piece of music tells us how long to play notes for, it also needs to tell us how long the silences should be and it does this by using rests.

There is an equivalent rest symbol for each note value you've already come across.

### HINTS & TIPS

Dots can also be added to rests, increasing their length by half.

◀ **Dotted crotchet rest (1 1/2 beats)**

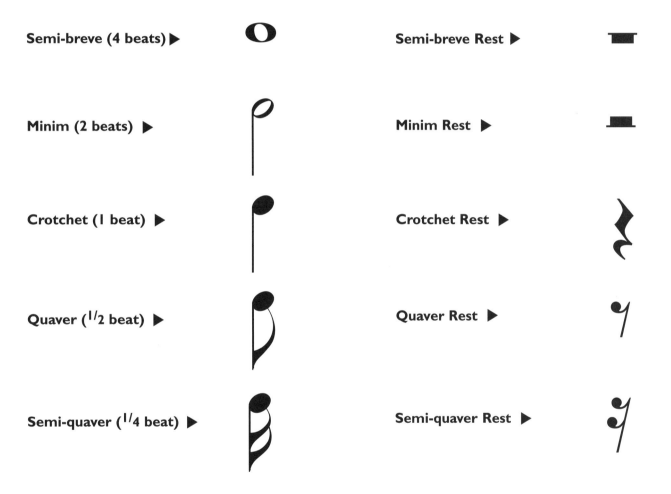

**Semi-breve (4 beats)** ▶

**Minim (2 beats)** ▶

**Crotchet (1 beat)** ▶

**Quaver (1/2 beat)** ▶

**Semi-quaver (1/4 beat)** ▶

**Semi-breve Rest** ▶

**Minim Rest** ▶

**Crotchet Rest** ▶

**Quaver Rest** ▶

**Semi-quaver Rest** ▶

Having practised reading a score and playing notes, you now need to get used to reading rests – in other words, *not* playing notes! The most important thing to remember is counting: rests can be confusing but try to keep to the beat even when you're not playing – and you should be OK.

If you have problems remembering which rest corresponds to which note, try writing the length of the rest, or the note symbol, underneath. Remember, each bar must add up to four beats, so with that in mind, you should be able to work out the length of each rest in this following example.

# Left-hand chords

So far the left hand has had nothing to do - but now all that's about to change!

## Harmonising

You can play tunes with your right hand – but in order to play your favourite songs, you'll need to be able to 'fill in' the sound a bit more, i.e. harmonise. This involves playing **chords** with your left hand. There are many different types of chords but we'll start with the **major chord**, which is the most common.

## The C major chord

The first chord we'll look at is **C major**. Looking at the diagram on the right, you'll see that some of the notes have been marked with black dots. Use your left hand to play these notes simultaneously.

The left hand needs to be comfortable as you play the chords and so the choice of fingers used to play the notes is important.

### HINTS & TIPS

**So what is a chord?**
*A chord is three or more notes played together - this could be three notes played by one hand or ten notes played by both hands!*

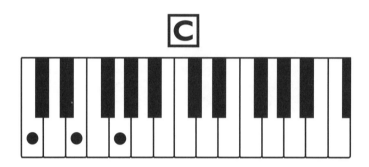

▼ **This is not the best way to play the chord of C major:**

▼ **You'll find that it feels more 'natural' to space out your fingers slightly while playing chords.**

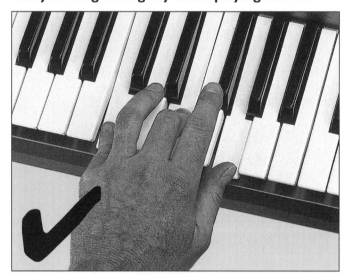

### HINTS & TIPS

◄ All the left-hand chords that we'll learn in this book will use the same section of the keyboard.

# Left-hand chords (continued)

L et's have a look at some more chords:

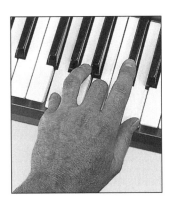

**G major**

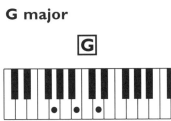

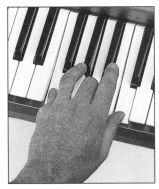

**F major**

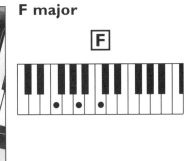

Now try the following chords which use sharps:

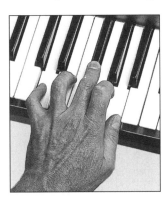

**D major**

**A major**

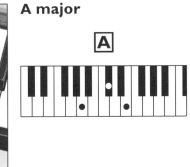

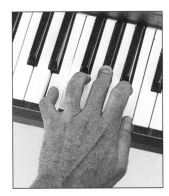

**E major**

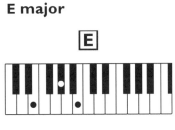

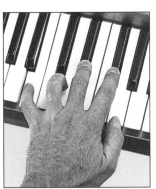

**B major**

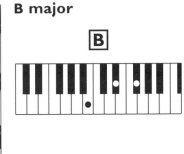

And now try these chords which use flats:

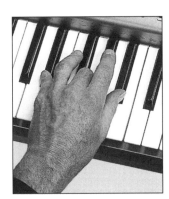

**E♭ major**

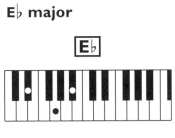

**B♭ major**

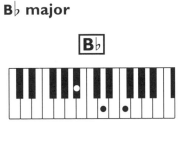

# Chord changes

Now let's try moving between the chords **C** and **F**, in three different ways:

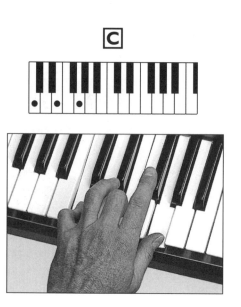

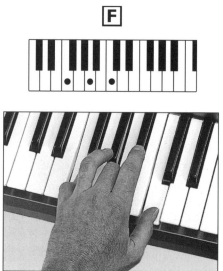

### ◀ Start with C major to F major:

You'll have noticed how your hand needed to move to get from one chord to the other.

The notes in a chord can be played in a different order - this is called an **inversion** – so your hand won't need to move as much and your playing will be much smoother.

### ▶ Now try it like this:

Try moving from **C major** to **F major** again and notice how much easier it is using a different shape for the **F** chord.

Again, we're using an **inversion** of the F chord, in order to make it easier to move from C. **Inversion** simply means that we've changed the order of the notes around, putting a different note at the bottom.

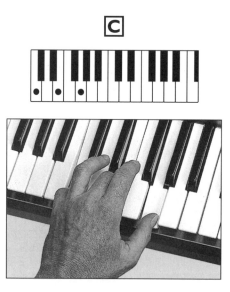

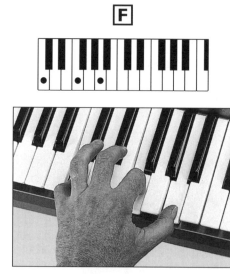

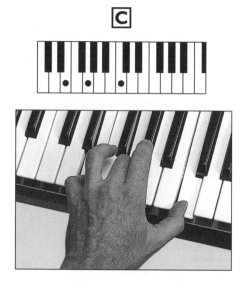

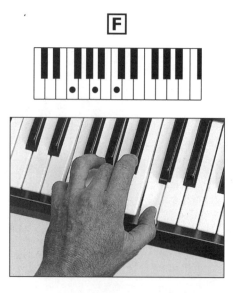

### ◀ Use an inversion

Here's another way of playing **C major** – an 'inversion'. Try these:

By using these two shapes, you should be able to change smoothly between the chords of **C** and **F**.

Let's now try moving between some different chords to get the left hand used to some different shapes.

You'll have to think more carefully now about where you're placing your fingers.

C

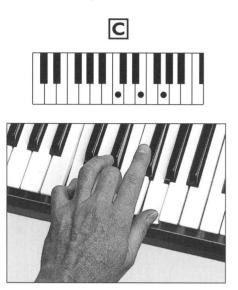

G

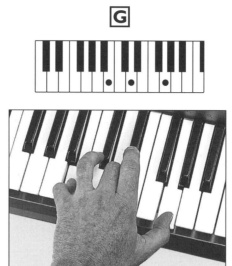

**◄ C major to G major**

First, try moving from **C major** (root position) to **G major** (second inversion). The change should be quite smooth.

**► F major to G major**

Notice how the chord 'shape' is exactly the same for both of these chords.

You can either keep your fingers in the same position when moving from **F** to **G**, and just move your hand, or you can try using different fingering for the **G** chord, as shown in our photo, to make the change smoother.

F

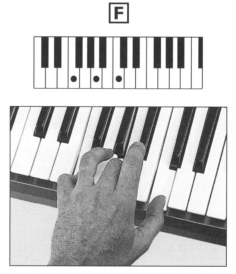

G

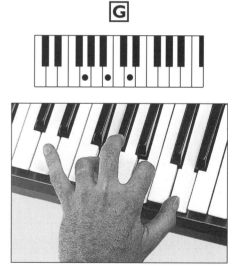

D

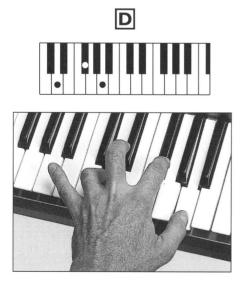

A

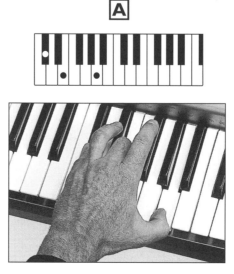

**◄ D major to A major**

The last chord change here is from **D major** to **A major**. Again, we're using an **inversion** of **A major**, in order to make the chord change easier and smoother.

# Three chord changes

Try these:

From **C major** to **F major** to **G major**:

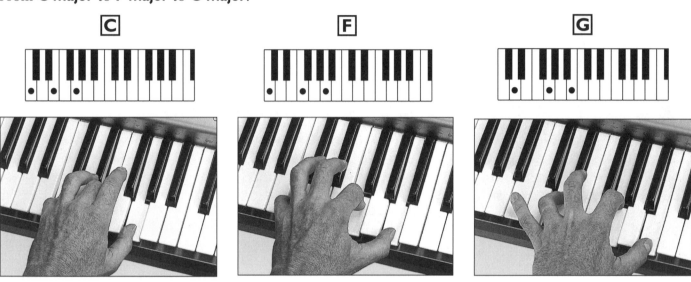

From **F major** to **G major** to **C major**:

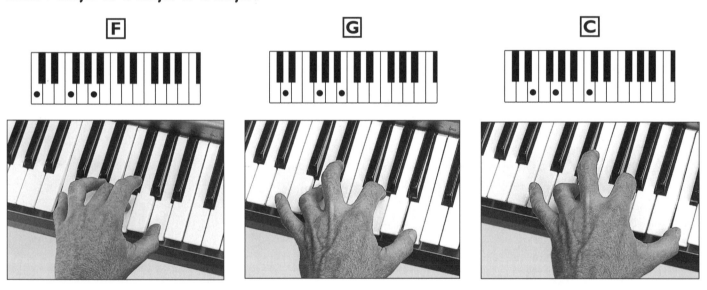

From **A major** to **D major** to **E major**:

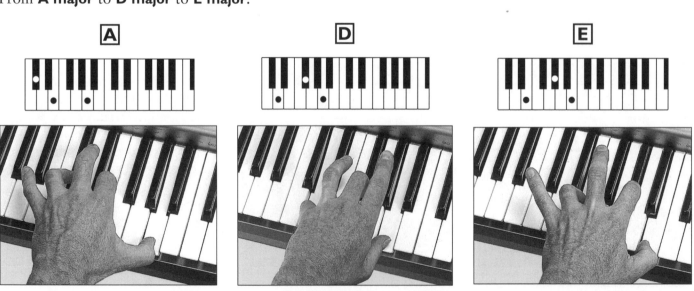

We are now ready for what keyboard playing is really all about - playing with both hands together! This means that the left hand will be moving from chord to chord whilst the right hand plays the tune or melody line.

Let's start with a very simple tune in the right hand and just one chord in the left hand so that you can get used to using both hands at the same time. You're already working with the sort of notes and chords which will allow you to start playing from The *Easiest Keyboard Collection!*

Try this piece in **C major**:

Now let's move on to a piece with two chords in the left hand. Remember to keep counting and try

and keep your playing steady. Start off slowly – and then gradually build up the speed.

# Using three and four chords

This next piece uses three chords:

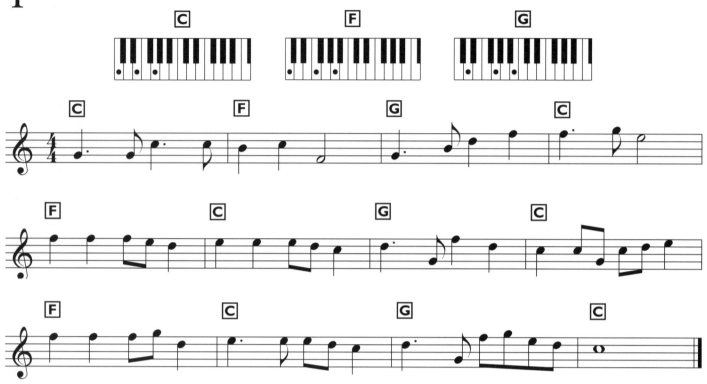

Now you are ready to move on to a piece using four chords. As before, count steadily and, with a bit of practice, you'll soon find this a piece of cake!

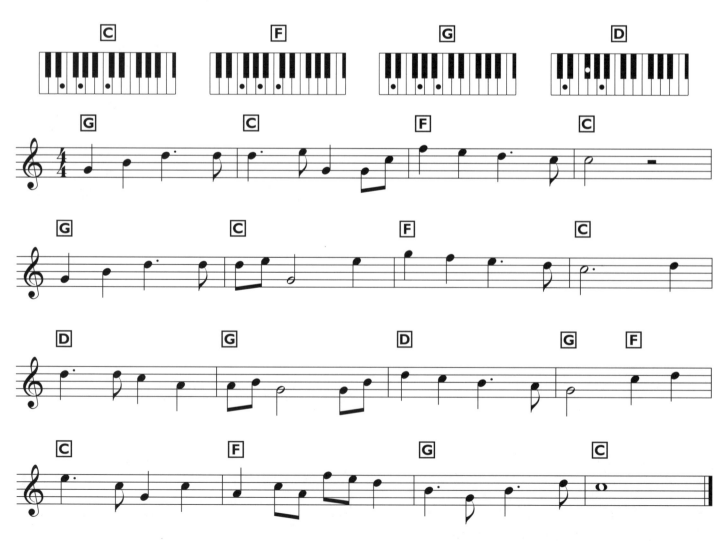

# Left-hand minor chords

The next chord we are going to look at is the **minor** chord. A minor chord has a sad and melancholy sound, unlike the major chord which is much brighter.

Listen to the sound of these chords:

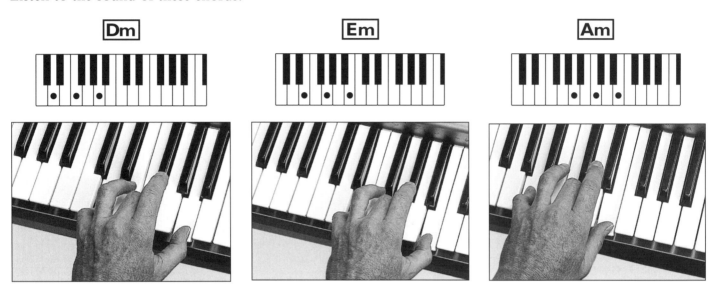

The following minor chords also use black notes:

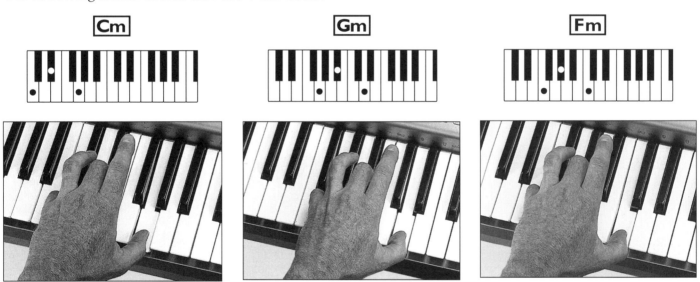

This minor chord uses only black notes:

---

### HINTS & TIPS

*The technical difference between **major** and **minor** chords is that the third note of the major scale is played a semi-tone lower (or 'flattened'), and this note is called the 'minor third'. It is this note which makes the minor chord sound sad.*

Now, let's try moving from one minor chord to another minor chord.

**Cm**

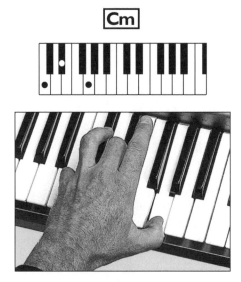

**Fm**

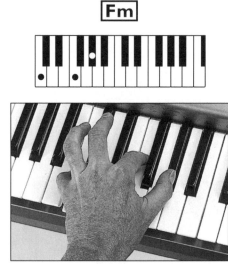

### ▶ Start with C minor to F minor:

Use fingers 5,3,1 for the **Cm** chord, and fingers 5,2,1 for the **Fm** chord. This will make the change much smoother (see the photos right).

### ▶ Now try moving from D minor to A minor.

Again, you'll find this chord change much easier if you follow our suggested fingering in the photograph, i.e: use fingers 4, 2 and 1 for the **D minor** chord, allowing you to move to **A minor** (using fingers 5, 3 and 1) much more smoothly.

**Dm**

**Am**

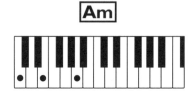

### ▼ Finally, try this change, which involves three chords.

The right fingering is crucial here. Why not try some alternative fingerings – it's important to find the way which is most comfortable for your fingers.

**Em**

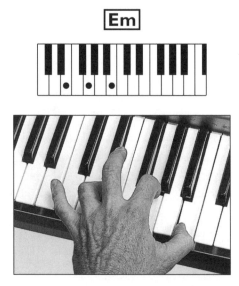

**Gm**

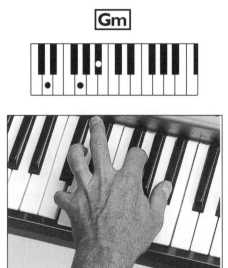

**Am**

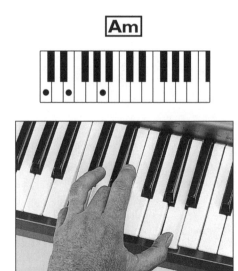

# Minor chords – both hands together

Now, let's try this short piece which uses two minor chords in the left hand, and a fairly simple melody in the right hand. Watch out for the Ab in bar 1 – that's the black note in between G and A.

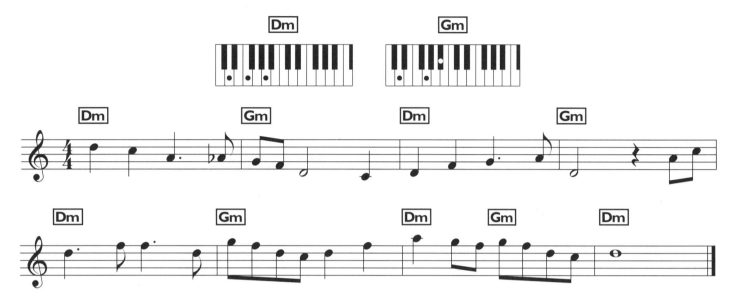

This next piece is in **C minor**, which uses three flats, and also features three left-hand chords. The melody might take a little practise – why not work on the left and right hands separately first, then put them together.

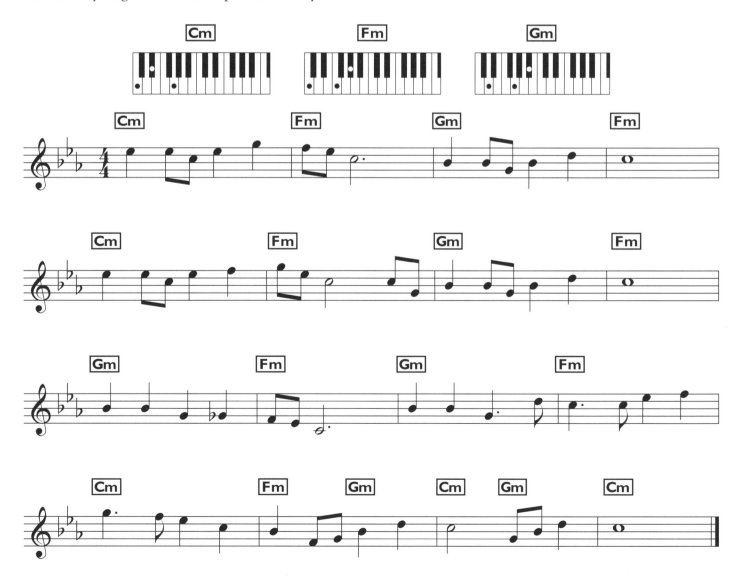

# Theme by Paganini

You're doing well! We have now looked at **rests**, left-hand **major** and **minor chords** and have started to play with both hands together.

This piece features many of the things you have learnt so far and is a chance to hear the progress you are making with your keyboard playing.

### HINTS & TIPS

*Familiarise yourself with the seven chords used in this piece before you try playing it with both hands together. Think about the chord progressions, and which fingers you should be using, before you get to the next chord. This is also a vital skill to develop in sight-reading and improvising.*

**Extract from 'Theme'**
by Niccolo Paganini

So far all the pieces of music you have played have been in 4/4 time, i.e. four beats to each bar. The technical term for this is the time signature and it is written at the beginning of a piece of music.

## 3/4 time

We are now going to look at a new time signature: 3/4 time.

Here are some of the ways a bar of 3/4 time can be made up:

As you might have guessed, this means three crotchet beats to each bar, and it is counted like this:

## 1-2-3/ 1-2-3/ 1-2-3/ 1-2-3/ etc.

As you try this count, emphasising the '1' of each bar, you will notice a swinging or swaying feel which is the main characteristic of 3/4 time. The classic example of this is the waltz, which is a dance in 3/4 time.

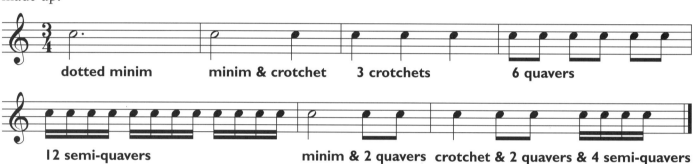

dotted minim     minim & crotchet     3 crotchets     6 quavers

12 semi-quavers     minim & 2 quavers    crotchet & 2 quavers & 4 semi-quavers

As you try the following piece, you will notice the difference in feel from the previous 4/4 pieces.

Counting is really important here – but remember to count to 3 in each bar rather than 4!

We have already seen that beats can be divided into parts so, for example, a crotchet can be divided into two quavers, as shown below.

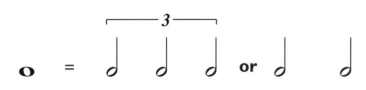

However, a beat can also be divided into three equal parts, and these are called **triplets**. This is shown on the music by a small '3' placed over or under the notes.

Any note can be divided into triplets – see the diagram on the right:

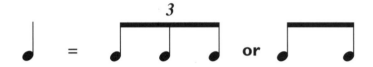

### Counting
The best way to approach this in $^4/4$ is to concentrate on playing the three notes within a count of 1. For **crotchet** triplets, this means you need to count two beats in a bar, and for **quaver** triplets, you can count the usual four.

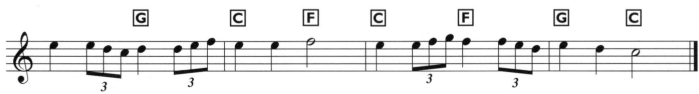

So far, the music we have looked at has been divided into bars with three or four beats to each bar. Although this is a convenient way of writing music it does give us a small problem – what happens if we want a note to sound for longer than one bar? Or, what happens if we want the final note of one bar to last into the first beat of the next bar? This problem is solved by using a **tie**.

A tie is a curved line joining two notes together across a bar, adding the length of the second note to the first note. Make sure you only strike the first note!

Tied notes can also be used within a bar if a note needs to be extended, as in this next example:

In this first example the **semi-breve** would be held for four bars (i.e. 16 beats):

In this example the tie joins a **minim** to a **crotchet** – making the tied note last for three beats. This also gives the music an off-beat, funky sound.

This piece features tied notes, so don't forget to keep your counting going as this will help with the notes that cross the bar lines.

Why not write the counts in underneath, if you're not sure to start with?

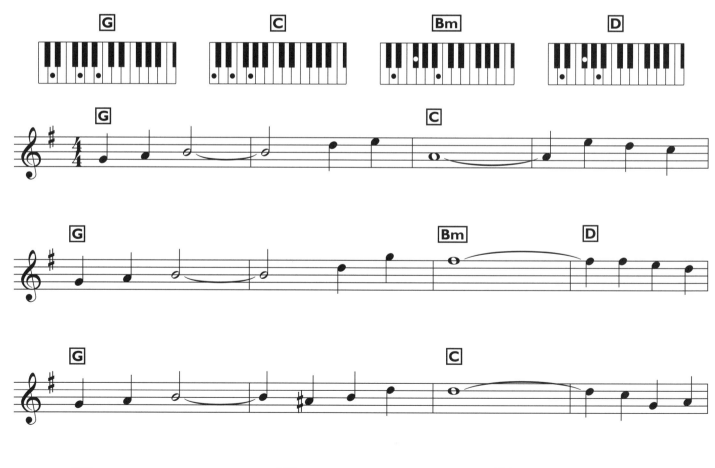

# 36 Dominant 7th chords

We are now going to look at another popular chord, often used in jazz and blues, called a **7**th. It's written like this – **C7**, **G7**, **D7** etc.

Often these chords will use four notes, which makes the chord sound more interesting and gives a fuller sound.

### HINTS & TIPS

*The chord is technically called a '**dominant 7th**' but it's abbreviated to simply 7. It is formed by adding the flattened seventh note of the major scale to the basic major chord. E.g: in C, this would be C, E, G, B♭.*

**C7**

Here's an example of a **7** chord. It uses C, E, G and B♭, but of course the notes don't have to be played in that order. You'll notice that the **7** chord has a very different feel to a straight major or minor chord – it sounds like it's 'going' somewhere.

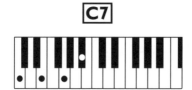

This next piece features **7**th chords. Try this, listening to the difference between the **7**th chords and the straight major or minor chords you've already learnt.

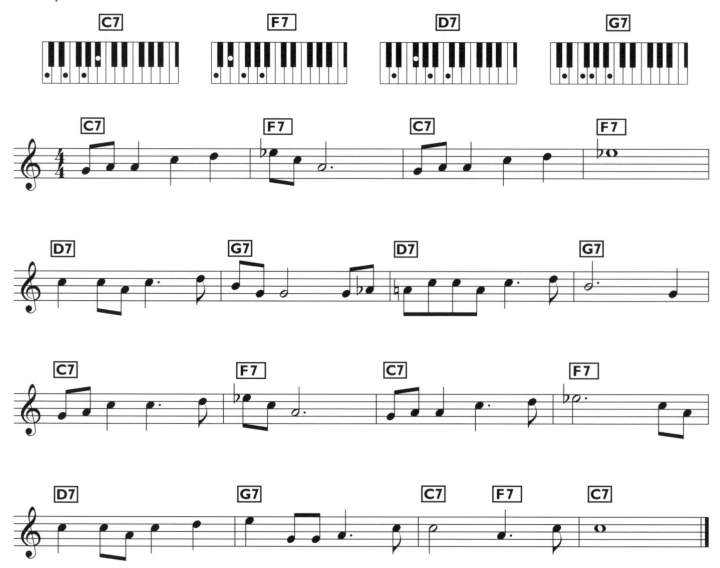

# Major 7th chords

This next chord is also a 7th chord but is called a **major 7** and is written like this – **Cmaj7, Gmaj7, Dmaj7** etc.

The **major 7** is made up of notes 1, 3, 5 and 7 of the major scale. In C, this would be C, E, G and B. It has a slightly more open feel than the dominant 7.

### C major 7

Here's an example of a **major 7** chord. Compare the difference in sound between **Cmaj7** and **C7**.

Try this next piece which features **major 7** chords:

# The House Of The Rising Sun

You've now learnt about **triplets**, **tied** notes, **dominant 7**th and **major 7**th chords. Here's a chance to use all of these in the next piece – which will also let you hear the progress you are making with your keyboard playing. Watch out for the chord changes – there are quite a few of them!

**The House Of The Rising Sun**

Traditional

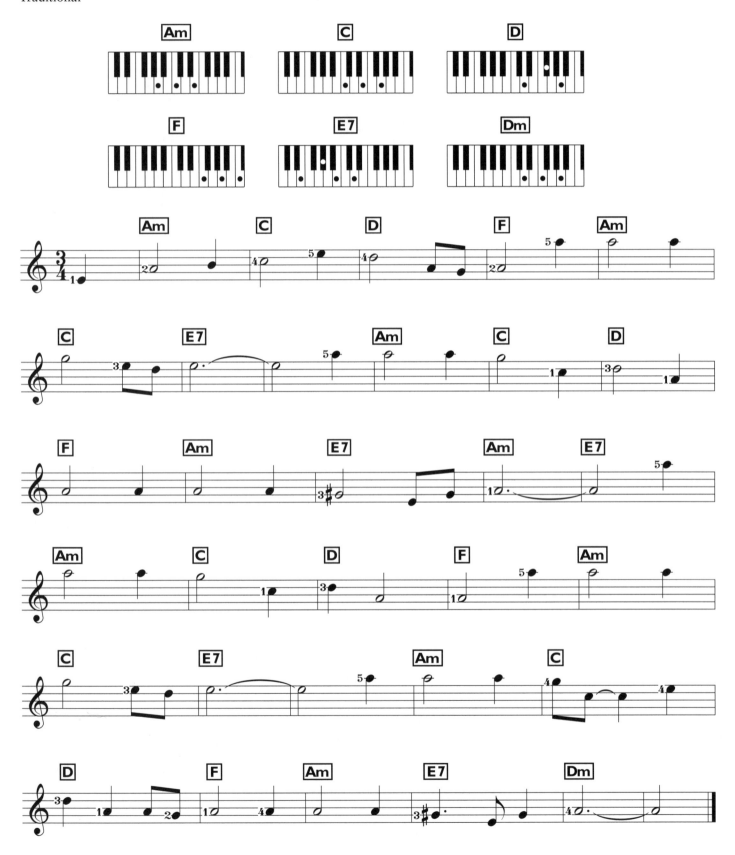

# More about time signatures

As we have already seen, the time signature is the two numbers written at the beginning of a piece of music and so far we have looked at $4/4$ and $3/4$.

## Other time signatures

However there are also a number of other time signatures, so it is worth having a look at what the two numbers actually mean.

The number on the top tells us how many beats are in a bar - so in $4/4$ there are four beats and in $3/4$ there are three beats.

The number on the bottom tells us what note length the beat will actually be and works like this:

**2** = minim beats

**4** = crotchet beats

**8** = quaver beats

So, $4/4$ literally means four **crotchet** beats in a bar.

Other than $6/8$ and $12/8$, which we will look at on the next page, here are the other most common time signatures:

$2/2$ which means two **minim** beats in a bar.

$2/4$ which means two **crotchet** beats in a bar.

$5/4$ is less common, and means five **crotchet** beats in a bar. Listen to Dave Brubeck's 'Take Five' for a good example of the feel of this time signature.

$3/8$ is also less common and means three **quaver** beats in a bar. It can sound like $3/4$, but a little more fast-paced.

## HINTS & TIPS

*Remember when dealing with time signatures, that the top number tells you **how many** beats are in the bar, and the bottom number tells you **what type** of beats they are.*

# 6/8 and 12/8 time

The time signatures 6/8 and 12/8 are popular in both classical and contemporary music.

6/8 means six **quaver** beats in a bar.

12/8 means twelve **quaver** beats in a bar.

At this point you might be wondering... 'If 6/8 is six quaver beats in a bar, and 3/4 is 3 crotchet beats in a bar, and three crotchets equals six quavers, then aren't 6/8 and 3/4 the same thing?'

Good question! The answer is that in 6/8 the quaver beats are usually 'grouped' into two

groups of three quavers (like triplets), and in 3/4, they would usually be 'grouped' into three groups of two quavers.

Also, in 3/4 there is a slight emphasis on the first beat of the bar, whereas in 6/8 the emphasis is on the first quaver of each 'group' – so it sounds like 2 main beats. Try counting or playing these:

So, 6/8 feels like it has two main beats (and 12/8 would have four) whereas 3/4 has three beats with

a slight emphasis on the first. To see what playing 6/8 is like, try the following piece:

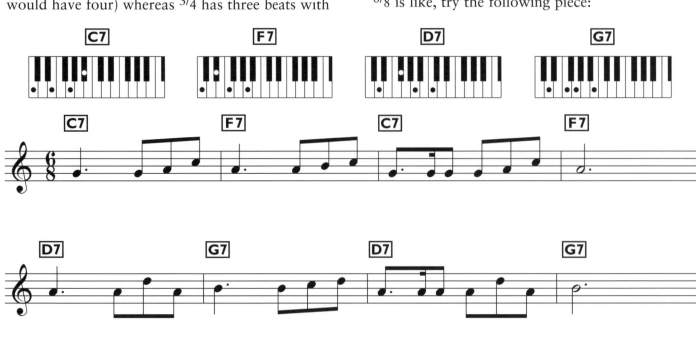

We are now going to look at one more **7**th chord – the **minor 7**th, which is written like this - **Cm7**, **Gm7**, **Dm7** etc.

As its name suggests, this chord simply adds a flattened 7th to a minor chord, but this addition makes the chord sound a little more interesting.

### Cm7

Here's an example of a **minor 7** chord. It's made up of notes 1, ♭3, 5, and ♭7 of the major scale. So in C, this is C, E♭, G and B♭. Why not compare the sound of this to the **C7** and **Cmajor7** chords on pages 36 and 37?

You're now ready to try this piece featuring **minor 7**th chords:

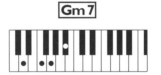

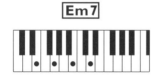

# Sus 4 chords

The last chord we are going to look at is the **suspended 4t**h chord and it is written like this – **Csus4, Gsus4, Dsus4** etc. This is basically a major chord with the third note replaced by the fourth.

It is called suspended because it creates a 'suspension' – a feeling of wanting to resolve, or move on to the next chord. This chord is usually simply referred to as a **sus4**.

**Csus4**

Here's **Csus4**. It uses notes 1, 4 and 5 of the major scale, so in C, this is C, F and G. The fingering shown makes it easy to resolve to the major chord by changing the F to an E.

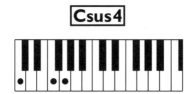

You can now try this piece featuring **sus 4** chords:

Well done! You're coming towards the end of this book, and you'll soon be able to play from the range of *Easiest Keyboard Collection* song books. You now have another chance to hear your progress as you try this piece which features some

more of the things you've learnt so far:

- **More time signatures, including** $^6/_8$ **and** $^3/_4$
- **The minor 7th**
- **The sus 4 chord**

## Extract from 'Greensleeves'

Traditional

# Keyboard sounds

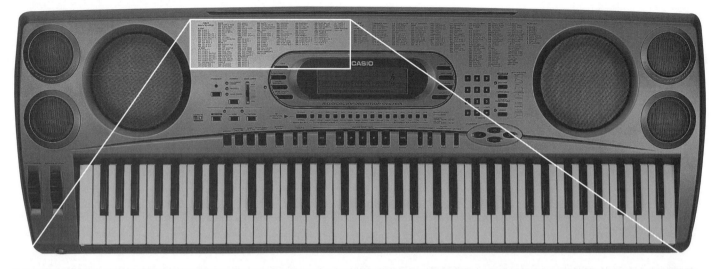

| 130 RHYTHMS | ROCK | | | | | | |
|---|---|---|---|---|---|---|---|
| | 020 SHUFFLE ROCK | 042 JUNGLE | 065 WALTZ 1 | 081 PASODOBLE | 093 BLUEGRASS | 105 BLUES BALLAD | 117 WALTZ 2 |
| 8 BEAT | 021 8 BEAT ROCK | 043 TECHNO | 066 FRENCH WALTZ | 082 REGGAE 1 | 094 COUNTRY | 106 MELLOW JAZZ | 118 WALTZ 3 |
| 000 8 BEAT 1 | 022 70'S ROCK | 044 RAP | 067 BALLROOM WALTZ | 083 REGGAE 2 | 095 50'S BALLAD | 107 JAZZ COMBO 2 | 119 WALTZ 4 |
| 001 8 BEAT 2 | 023 80'S ROCK | 045 DANCE FLOOR | 068 VIENNESE WALTZ | 084 BEGUINE | 096 HAWAIIAN | 108 RAGTIME | USER RHYTHM |
| 002 8 BEAT BALLAD 1 | 024 HEAVY METAL | 046 HOUSE | 069 TANGO | 085 SKA | 097 BROADWAY | 109 BOOGIE-WOOGIE | 120~129 |
| 003 8 BEAT BALLAD 2 | 025 R&B | 047 DANCE | LATIN I | 086 EURO FOX | 098 ADANI | FOR PIANO II | |
| 004 8 BEAT BALLAD 3 | 026 ROCK | 048 OLDIES POP | 070 BOSSA NOVA 1 | 087 BALLROOM FOX | 099 BALADI | 110 ARPEGGIO 1 | |
| 005 PIANO ROCK | 027 50'S R&R | 049 OLDIES SHUFFLE | 071 BOSSA NOVA 2 | 088 QUICKSTEP | FOR PIANO I | 111 ARPEGGIO 2 | |
| 006 POP ROCK 1 | 028 NEW ORLNS R&R | JAZZ | 072 RHUMBA 1 | 089 FOX TROT | 100 PIANO BALLAD 1 | 112 ARPEGGIO 3 | |
| 007 POP ROCK 2 | 029 TWIST | 050 BIG BAND 1 | 073 RHUMBA 2 | VARIOUS II | 101 PIANO BALLAD 2 | 113 PIANO BALLAD 4 | |
| 008 70'S 8 BEAT | POPS I | 051 BIG BAND 2 | 074 MAMBO | 090 FAST GOSPEL | 102 PIANO BALLAD 3 | 114 6/8 MARCH | |
| 009 60'S 8 BEAT | 030 MODERN R&B | 052 SWING 1 | 075 SAMBA 1 | 091 SLOW GOSPEL | 103 EP BALLAD 1 | 115 MARCH 1 | |
| 16 BEAT | 031 POP | 053 SWING 2 | 076 SAMBA 2 | 092 CHICAGO BLUES | 104 EP BALLAD 2 | 116 2 BEAT | |
| 010 16 BEAT 1 | 032 POP SHUFFLE | 054 SWING 3 | 077 BOLERO | | | | |
| 011 16 BEAT 2 | 033 80'S POP | 055 SLOW SWING | 078 CHA-CHA-CHA | | | | |
| 012 16 BEAT SHUFFLE | 034 SOUL POP | 056 ORCH SWING | 079 MERENGUE | | | | |
| 013 16 BEAT BALLAD 1 | 035 WORLD POP | 057 JAZZ COMBO 1 | LATIN II/VARIOUS I | | | | |
| 014 16 BEAT BALLAD 2 | 036 SLOW ROCK | 058 JAZZ WALTZ 1 | 080 SALSA | | | | |
| 015 16 BEAT BALLAD 3 | 037 6/8 BALLAD | 059 JAZZ WALTZ 2 | | | | | |
| 016 16 BEAT SOUL | 038 SOUL BALLAD | EUROPEAN | | | | | |
| 017 BIG BAND ROCK | 039 ROCK WALTZ | 060 POLKA 1 | | | | | |
| 018 FUNKY POP 1 | POPS II | 061 POLKA 2 | | | | | |
| 019 FUNKY POP 2 | 040 70'S DISCO | 062 MARCH 1 | | | | | |
| | 041 80'S DISCO | 063 MARCH 2 | | | | | |
| | | 064 MARCH 3 | | | | | |

Your electronic keyboard will give you access to a wide range of voices which you can select from to play the music of your choice.

Books in the *Easiest Keyboard Collection* suggest a suitable voice at the beginning of each piece, together with a recommended tempo and rhythm preset. But you don't have to stick to these – experiment!

The characteristic sound of a voice, whether it is a real instrument or a synthesised keyboard sound, influences the way it is used. So, we're now going to look at some voices and think about the most effective way to use them.

### Keyboard Instruments
Instruments like **piano, electric piano, organ, harpsichord, clavinet** etc. are included in this section. They are played with both hands, and so can be selected both for left-hand accompaniment, and also for playing the tune with the right hand. Piano sounds are particularly good to practise with because they give a clear, clean sound so that you can easily hear the notes you are playing.

### Guitars
**Acoustic, steel** and **jazz** guitars will work for both left-hand accompaniment and right-hand melody. **Bass** guitar sounds are for the left-hand part but will usually only work if you select a single-note accompaniment setting rather than chords.

### Orchestral Solo Instruments
There are a number of orchestral instruments that work well when playing the right-hand melody, e.g. **violin, cello, saxophone, trumpet, french horn, clarinet, flute, recorder** etc. It is simply a matter of personal taste as to which instrument you select... so, try them all out!

### Sections and Pads
These are voices which give a full, rich blend of sound and might be **string, brass** or **choral** sections or synthesised sounds which are often called **pads** or given descriptive names e.g. **Brightness, Atmosphere.** These voices tend to be used for left-hand accompaniment although they can be used to play a right-hand melody - again, let your ears be the judge!

Your electronic keyboard gives you the chance to experiment with voices and sounds, and then use them in a way that works for you. A piece of music played with a piano taking the melody can be transformed by changing the voice, so start pressing those buttons!

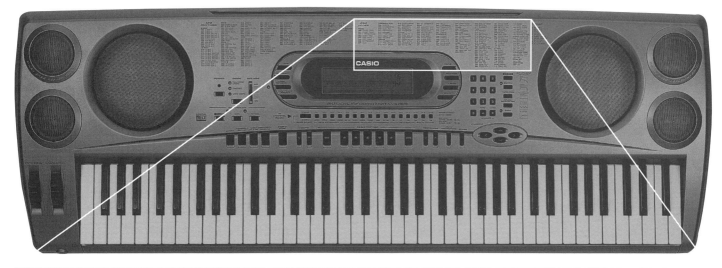

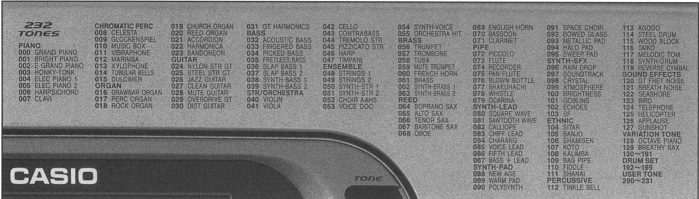

| 232 TONES | | | | | | | |
|---|---|---|---|---|---|---|---|
| **PIANO** | **CHROMATIC PERC** | **019** CHURCH ORGAN | **042** CELLO | **054** SYNTH-VOICE | **069** ENGLISH HORN | **091** SPACE CHOIR | **113** AGOGO |
| **000** GRAND PIANO | **008** CELESTA | **020** REED ORGAN | **043** CONTRABASS | **055** ORCHESTRA HIT | **070** BASSOON | **092** BOWED GLASS | **114** STEEL DRUM |
| **001** BRIGHT PIANO | **009** GLOCKENSPIEL | **021** ACCORDION | **BASS** | **BRASS** | **071** CLARINET | **093** METALLIC PAD | **115** WOOD BLOCK |
| **002** E GRAND PIANO | **010** MUSIC BOX | **022** HARMONICA | **032** ACOUSTIC BASS | **056** TRUMPET | **PIPE** | **094** HALO PAD | **116** TAIKO |
| **003** HONKY-TONK | **011** VIBRAPHONE | **023** BANDONEON | **033** FINGERED BASS | **057** TROMBONE | **072** PICCOLO | **095** SWEEP PAD | **117** MELODIC TOM |
| **004** ELEC PIANO 1 | **012** MARIMBA | **GUITAR** | **034** PICKED BASS | **058** TUBA | **073** FLUTE | **SYNTH-SFX** | **118** SYNTH-DRUM |
| **005** ELEC PIANO 2 | **013** XYLOPHONE | **024** NYLON STR GT | **035** FRETLESS BASS | **059** MUTE TRUMPET | **074** RECORDER | **096** RAIN DROP | **119** REVERSE CYMBAL |
| **006** HARPSICHORD | **014** TUBULAR BELLS | **025** STEEL STR GT | **036** SLAP BASS 1 | **060** FRENCH HORN | **075** PAN FLUTE | **097** SOUNDTRACK | **SOUND EFFECTS** |
| **007** CLAVI | **015** DULCIMER | **026** JAZZ GUITAR | **037** SLAP BASS 2 | **061** BRASS | **076** BLOWN BOTTLE | **098** CRYSTAL | **120** GT FRET NOISE |
| | **ORGAN** | **027** CLEAN GUITAR | **038** SYNTH-BASS 1 | **062** SYNTH-BRASS 1 | **077** SHAKUHACHI | **099** ATMOSPHERE | **121** BREATH NOISE |
| | **016** DRAWBAR ORGAN | **028** MUTE GUITAR | **039** SYNTH-BASS 2 | **063** SYNTH-BRASS 2 | **078** WHISTLE | **100** BRIGHTNESS | **122** SEASHORE |
| | **017** PERC ORGAN | **029** OVERDRIVE GT | **STR/ORCHESTRA** | **REED** | **079** OCARINA | **101** GOBLINS | **123** BIRD |
| | **018** ROCK ORGAN | **030** DIST GUITAR | **040** VIOLIN | **064** SOPRANO SAX | **SYNTH-LEAD** | **102** ECHOES | **124** TELEPHONE |
| | | **031** GT HARMONICS | **041** VIOLA | **065** ALTO SAX | **080** SQUARE WAVE | **103** SF | **125** HELICOPTER |
| | | **BASS** | **ENSEMBLE** | **066** TENOR SAX | **081** SAWTOOTH WAVE | **ETHNIC** | **126** APPLAUSE |
| | | **032** ACOUSTIC BASS | **048** STRINGS 1 | **067** BARITONE SAX | **082** CALLIOPE | **104** SITAR | **127** GUNSHOT |
| | | **033** FINGERED BASS | **049** STRINGS 2 | **068** OBOE | **083** CHIFF LEAD | **105** BANJO | **VARIATION TONE** |
| | | **034** PICKED BASS | **050** SYNTH-STR 1 | | **084** CHARANG | **106** SHAMISEN | **128** OCTAVE PIANO |
| | | **035** FRETLESS BASS | **051** SYNTH-STR 2 | | **085** VOICE LEAD | **107** KOTO | **129** BREATHY SAX |
| | | **036** SLAP BASS 1 | **052** CHOIR AAHS | | **086** FIFTH LEAD | **108** KALIMBA | **130~191** |
| | | **037** SLAP BASS 2 | **053** VOICE DOO | | **087** BASS + LEAD | **109** BAG PIPE | **DRUM SET** |
| | | **038** SYNTH-BASS 1 | | | **SYNTH-PAD** | **110** FIDDLE | **192~199** |
| | | **039** SYNTH-BASS 2 | | | **088** NEW AGE | **111** SHANAI | **USER TONE** |
| | | | | | **089** WARM PAD | **PERCUSSIVE** | **200~231** |
| | | | | | **090** POLYSYNTH | **112** TINKLE BELL | |

Your electronic keyboard will also provide you with a number of preset rhythm accompaniments and the facility to alter the tempo, i.e. speed them up or slow them down.

## Tempo

Being able to adjust the tempo is very useful when first playing a piece or practising a section of a piece that you might find difficult – by slowing the tempo down you can give yourself a little more time to think about what's coming up, and then as confidence grows you can gradually speed up again.

The way the tempo is shown is as follows:

♩ = 120

This means that the tempo is 120 **crotchet** beats per minute (this is often written as 120 B.P.M).

## Rhythm

There are obviously countless different rhythms which can accompany music but in contemporary music they tend to fit into certain categories:

## Rock/Pop

These are generally $4/4$ or $2/4$ time signatures and are the most common in contemporary pop music. These styles are all characterised by a strong four-beat feel with a snare drum emphasising beats 2 and 4.

## Dance/Funk/Disco

These tend to be built on four strong beats from the bass drum, a heavy snare on beats 2 and 4 with more intricate hi-hat cymbals and percussion parts layered on the top.

## Latin

This includes styles such as Samba, Bossa Nova, Rumba, Cha-Cha etc. These usually feature intricate percussion parts and are great fun to play along with!

## Swing/Shuffle

Many jazz and blues style pieces use these rhythms and the tempos will range from slow, lazy blues to fast, toe-tapping shuffles.

## $6/8$ and Triplets

This one is fairly obvious - these presets need to be selected if the piece is in $6/8$, $12/8$ or is written using triplets. Selecting the wrong preset will soon show you why!

Rhythm is a critical ingredient of music so, having read about them, now start experimenting for yourself.

# The Entertainer

Playing the keyboard should be enjoyable and rewarding, and hopefully your journey through the pages of this book has already been an enjoyable one! Let's just think back on where our musical journey has taken us.

## What you've learnt

We've worked on the keyboard playing position for the hands and body; we've learnt how to read music and play the notes on the page, and we've thought about key signatures and time signatures, dotted notes and triplets, rests and ties, major, minor, 7th and suspended chords.

You are now well equipped to start playing from the extensive range of books in The *Easiest Keyboard Collection* series (take a look at page 48 for a selection of titles).

## Your final piece

Here's a final piece for you to try, which should test all of your newly-found musical ability. Well done on the progress you have made in this book – and keep up the good work!

**The Entertainer**
By Scott Joplin

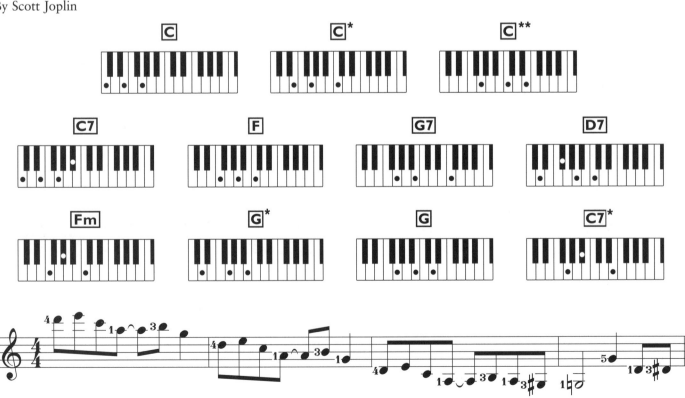

# EASIEST KEYBOARD COLLECTION

Easy-to-play melody line arrangements for all keyboards with chord symbols and lyrics. Suggested registration, rhythm and tempo are included for each song together with keyboard diagrams showing left-hand chord voicings used.

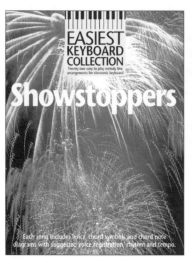

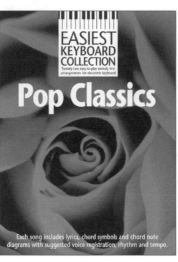

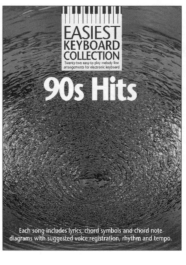

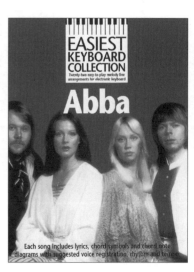

## Showstoppers

Consider Yourself (Oliver!), Do You Hear The People Sing? (Les Misérables), I Know Him So Well (Chess), Maria (West Side Story), Smoke Gets In Your Eyes (Roberta) and 17 more big stage hits.
**Order No. AM944218**

## Pop Classics

A Whiter Shade Of Pale (Procol Harum), Bridge Over Troubled Water (Simon & Garfunkel), Crocodile Rock (Elton John) and 19 more classic hit songs, including Hey Jude (The Beatles), Imagine (John Lennon), and Massachusetts (The Bee Gees).
**Order No. AM944196**

## 90s Hits

Over 20 of the greatest hits of the 1990s, including Always (Bon Jovi), Fields Of Gold (Sting), Have I Told You Lately (Rod Stewart), One Sweet Day (Mariah Carey), Say You'll Be There (Spice Girls), and Wonderwall (Oasis).
**Order No. AM944229**

## Abba

A great collection of 22 Abba hit songs. Includes: Dancing Queen, Fernando, I Have A Dream, Mamma Mia, Super Trouper, Take A Chance On Me, Thank You For The Music, The Winner Takes It All, and Waterloo.
**Order No. AM959860**

## Also available...

**Ballads**, Order No. AM952116
**The Beatles**, Order No. NO90686
**Boyzone**, Order No. AM958331
**Broadway**, Order No. AM952127
**Celine Dion**, Order No. AM959850
**Chart Hits**, Order No. AM952083
**Christmas**, Order No. AM952105
**Classic Blues**, Order No. AM950697
**Classics**, Order No. AM952094

**The Corrs**, Order No. AM959849
**Elton John**, Order No. AM958320
**Film Themes**, Order No. AM952050
**Hits of the 90s**, Order No. AM955780
**Jazz Classics**, Order No. AM952061
**Love Songs**, Order No. AM950708
**Pop Hits**, Order No. AM952072
**60s Hits**, Order No. AM955768
**80s Hits**, Order No. AM955779

**...plus many more!**